May you catch every star
you chase!

Byron M Phillips
August 26, 2010

STARS TO CHASE

Adventures in Rhyme
by Byron von Rosenberg

For Sharon
the star I chase
and the one who chases me!

With special appreciation to
Alyene Pierot
Gene von Rosenberg
Marjorie von Rosenberg

MAY YOUR LIPS ALWAYS BE LONG ENOUGH

May your lips always be long enough
To kiss the ones you love.
May your skies always be bright enough
To lift your eyes above.
May your hands always be strong enough
To hold on to what's good
Yet wise enough to let things go
When your heart says that you should.
May your feet always be sure enough
To find the narrow way
And kind enough to those you love
To bring you home someday.
May your heart always have courage
Enough to carry on
When hands and feet have failed
And all your strength is gone.
May your spirit then be bold enough
To look to that bright sky
And fill your soul with faith enough
To give you wings to fly!

Stars to Chase
Copyright ©2010 Byron von Rosenberg
All rights reserved.

Cover and Interior Design by Red Mountain Creations

Packaged by Red Mountain Creations
P.O. Box 172
High Ridge, MO 63049
www.idontwanttokissallama.com

Publisher's Cataloguing-in-Publication Data
(Provided by Cassidy Cataloguing Services, Inc.)

Von Rosenberg, Byron.

   Stars to chase : adventures in rhyme / by Byron von Rosenberg. --
High Ridge, MO : Red Mountain Creations, c2010.

      p. ; cm.

      ISBN: 978-0-9759858-8-5
      Includes author's notes on each poem.

      1. American poetry. 2. Humorous poetry, American. 3. Fables,
   American. I. Title.

PS3622.O67 S73 2010
811.6--dc22   1005

Printed in South Korea.

TABLE OF CONTENTS

STARS TO CHASE

I woke up this morning
Lost in outer space
And everything I ever knew
Was gone without a trace.
What to do? I did not know
For all was new to me,
And I remember thinking
What a strange place this was to be.
But I shook the twinkle off a star,
Caught a comet by the tail,
Stretched the rings of Saturn
And used them as a sail.

And even though there is no wind
In outer space to blow
Imagination took me everywhere
I could ever want to go.
I didn't need a ticket
To buy myself a ride
For the greatest of adventures
Is what goes on inside.
There are no limits in my mind
Or in yours either, friend,
So think those thoughts you're thinking
When you have some time to spend.
And if you should ever catch me
In my old familiar place
Remember that, inside my head,
I've still got stars to chase!

THE BED SHEET PARACHUTE

There was not a tree he couldn't climb
For miles and miles around
And it's said that little Leon
Never liked it on the ground.
One day his friends came calling
And hollered up the tree,
"Why don't you ride this bed sheet down
And tell us what you see?
You'd better do it, Leon!
There ain't no turning back!"
Such taunts can lead to pain
When it's common sense you lack.
Leon grabbed the corners
And leapt off of the limb.
If the bed sheet hadn't tangled,
There'd be nothing left of him.

When his father found him later
He was still quite badly stuck
And told him he should say his fate
Was, "Stupidity! Not bad luck."
So no matter what the pressure is
To succumb to such a dare
Remember the bed sheet parachute
And my advice,

"BEWARE!"

SHAKESPEARE FROG

He couldn't get the part.
He was too short for Romeo
So he tried out for Juliet
To get into the show.
It took a lot of makeup
But he finally looked okay
And decided he would pull a stunt
To blow the crowd away.

"I'll leap into my lover's arms
From atop the balcony
So when people think of Juliet
They will remember me!"
He had them build a platform
One hundred stories high
Neglecting one important fact
And that is: Frogs can't fly!

Shakespeare Frog! Oh, Shakespeare Frog!
We shall ne'er forget
For there never was a braver
Nor a flatter Juliet!

NO TV

If there were no TV
I think of all the things I'd see:
A flower bloom, a bird in flight.
Without TV I even might
Go outside of my front door
Where I could see a whole lot more.
People going all about!
Why I could even venture out
On a walk or in my car
But I'll never know just how far
I might have, could have, should have gone
'Cause I've still got the TV on!

CLUTTER

I wish there were
Some words to utter
To help get rid
Of all this clutter.
Bags and boxes
Everywhere
On the sofa
And the chair.
Cans and bottles
Gotta go!
Clean and sparkly!
Make it so.
Clutter's gone
Just like that!
But where I wonder
Is the cat?

OLD CHEESE

When I woke up this morning
My stomach said, "Eat!"
And my tongue said, "I want more
Than mushy oat bran or wheat!"
And so I went searching
In my refrigerator
And found some old cheese
Down deep in its core.
The date was expired.
It was sixteen months old
But I got out a knife
And scraped off the mold.
It looked a lot better
And tasted like new
But I was still hungry
So I ate the rest, too.
Now some folks might call that
Stupid or dumb
But you're holding your stomach.
Are you hungry?

WANT SOME?

THE TALKING FEET

I had a very weird dream.
My feet began to speak!
They complained about their bunions
And how my ankles creak.
They said my shoes were fitted
At least a size too small
And demanded a massage
Or they wouldn't walk at all.
They asked for thicker socks
To stay warm in icy weather
And sandals for the summertime
Instead of wearing leather.
When I finally woke
I took my morning walk
Thankful for my pair of feet
And glad that they can't talk.

THE PIG AND THE POODLE

I have a pig and a poodle
I keep in the house and sty.
It's the poodle that stays in the house
With the pig left to wonder why
It has to stay on the outside
In the rain, the heat, and the snow,
While I pamper the powderpuff poodle
To take to the kennel club show.
But it really shouldn't be jealous
For an indoor visit awaits,
At breakfast tomorrow morning
And we're using the best china plates!

PINCHING THE DINOSAUR

Have you ever tried to pinch
An angry dinosaur?
A caveman told me once
It was quite an awesome chore.
The reason that he did it
Was just to hear them roar
But I don't think he pinches
Or hears them anymore.

JUAN PABLO MADRID

This is the tale of Juan Pablo Madrid
Who amazed us all with the things that he did.
He took on the rapids at Niagara Falls,
Climbed and rappelled on China's Great Walls.
In all that he did he surely was brave
But what mattered most was the love that he gave.
Love of life and the trust of his friends,
The good in these gifts just never ends.
So on top of a mountain or sailing the sea
In every adventure I'll remember J. P.
For courage and valor he had in excess
And for his example I carry no less.
Truly he was a magnificent man
Whose deeds proclaimed loudly these words:
"Yes! I can!"

THE PIG HAS WINGS

The pig has wings.
They're little things
But high up in the air it swings
And I think of all the many kings
Who would have given crowns and rings
If they could rise up as on strings
Like the little pig with wings.

PEANUT BUTTER PETE:
THE SHOWDOWN WITH SNAKE OIL SAM

From the morning train in old Lampassas
Stepped Snake Oil Sam with his bottles and glasses.
"Friends!" he called. "Taste the oil of the snake
If your tummy's sick or your tooth's got an ache.
You can trust me! This remedy's real!
Bring what you've got and I'll make you a deal."
The weather was hot and the people were sweating
And what sense they had they all were forgetting.
They gave Sam their money, their ducks and their chickens.
The best of their crops – Old Sam got the pickin's.
But Peter PB didn't swallow the scam
And at the top of his lungs he said, "Now listen up, Sam!
Your tongue is smooth and your snake oil is slick
But that stuff's gonna make all these poor people sick.
When folks need a boost here's what I say:
You'll always feel better with PB and J!"

But Sam's temper grew hot and his face turned all red.
He snorted and shouted and here's what he said.
"These people don't want that sticky old stuff!
My oil is so good, you can't have enough!"

He opened his mouth and took a big swallow,
Then the whole jug and two more to follow.
All of a sudden he put his hand to his throat
And the noise that he made sounded just like a goat.
He started to shake then he trembled and fell
So Pete took him to jail to rest for a spell.
Sam tossed and he turned for twenty-three days
'Til he finally came out of his snakey oiled haze.
And the doctor who spent three weeks at his side
Said, "With regular medicine Sam would have died!
But Pete brought him a sandwich to eat for each meal.
That made Sam smile which helped him to heal."
Better in body and spirit was Sam
Who told all the town folk, "Oh, how grateful I am!
I got to eat gobs of Pete's peanut butter!
When I think of my snake oil it just makes me shudder!
Here are your crops, your chickens, your ducks!
You can have them all back, as well as your bucks."
They liked him so much they asked him to stay
And the friends that he made are still good to this day.
So when you need a pal, here's what to say,

"Sit down.

Have some milk –

and a PB and J!"

THE FIRST DAY BACK

I hate to get up in the morning
On the very first day of school.
I spent the whole summer playing
Without following one single rule.
But now those days are over
And I'm finding my way to my room.
With each step I'm feeling a sense
Of impending and awful doom.
I pause to ponder a question
As I put my hand to the door:
If this is what my life has become,
Do I want to live anymore?
I accept my fate with a sigh
For all good things must pass,
Walk in, put my books on the desk
And say, "Welcome! Good morning, class!"

I DON'T LIKE COFFEE!

I don't like coffee!
I don't like tea!
They just don't taste
That good to me.
I won't drink 'em!
Not one sip.
If they're too hot
They'll burn my lip!
Why'd they make
Drinks so bitter?
It tastes like they
Used kitty litter!
But it's so hard
To get up.
Think I'll have
A second cup!

THE ALGEBRA POEM

Algebra, algebra!
Do you know the answer? Duh!
x and y and z and q!
Look at how my problems grew!
Should I times it or divide
Or add a bit to either side?
What kind of person writes this stuff?
Weren't fractions bad enough?
Stick to numbers! Can the words!
Algebra is for the birds!

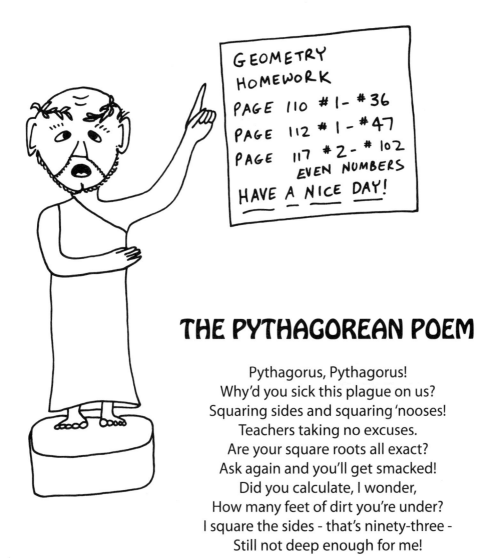

GEOMETRY
HOMEWORK
PAGE 110 #1 - #36
PAGE 112 #1 - #47
PAGE 117 #2 - #102
EVEN NUMBERS
HAVE A NICE DAY!

THE PYTHAGOREAN POEM

Pythagorus, Pythagorus!
Why'd you sick this plague on us?
Squaring sides and squaring 'nooses!
Teachers taking no excuses.
Are your square roots all exact?
Ask again and you'll get smacked!
Did you calculate, I wonder,
How many feet of dirt you're under?
I square the sides - that's ninety-three -
Still not deep enough for me!

CHASE THE BALL

My doggie likes to chase a ball
Outside in the snow.
She will chase it down the hill
As far as I can throw.
She doesn't care how cold it is!
(It's minus ten you know.)
But my doggie always loves this game!
Hey, now! Where'd she go?

SHARKS TO CHASE

I chased a shark the other day.
I thought it might be fun to play.
But it turned 'round and opened wide
And – just like that! – I was inside.
Life's like that when you live on credit
So take your card out – NOW! – and shred it!

OUR EAGLE

He's been stretching wings
Since the day he first breathed air
And every time he conquered one
He'd find another dare.
One more challenge to pursue
And chase it to the end
– His fierce determination! –
On that we could depend.
And now those wings are ready!
Our son is fully grown.
He has felt his freedom now
And to such heights he's flown.
And on this day and from this place
His journey starts anew
And though we can't go with him
The path he chose is true.
Honor, courage, faith,
He carries these things high.
Our son flies as an eagle!
There are no limits in his sky.
And so we proudly watch
As he rises on those wings
In thanks and admiration
For our son who does these things.

THEREIN WAS THE DAWN

He'd never spent so much time
So far away from home
Where the body and the spirit
Each had room to roam.
And somewhere on a mountainside
Way off the beaten track
A boy realized he was a man
And there was no turning back.
It might have been the eagle
High in the azure blue,
Advising him his set of wings
Must make his dreams come true.
It could have been the bear
That brushed the tent at night,
Reminding him to treasure
The gift of morning light.
And it might have been the sunrise
That crept up mountain slopes
That said to him great deeds would come
If he'd act upon his hopes.
And so he did and followed
That light up to the peaks
And now he knows that with his best
He can reach the goals he seeks.
He's traveled many miles since then
As days have come and gone
But a man awoke as daylight broke
And therein was the dawn.

IT'S TOO SMALL

It's too small but he still wears it,
Fading, but he doesn't care.
In fact, I think, of all he has
It's his favorite thing to wear.
He wore it every day at camp,
Made me wash it every night.
Wasn't that just yesterday?
How did it get so tight?
A craft he made sits on his shelf,
His very own creation.
It was fun to watch him work,
So full of concentration.
He shot a bow and arrow
And even learned to swim
But the friendships that he made
Still mean the most to him.
I have a shirt just like his
And though it's fading, too,
It reminds of times together
And those great days we knew.
So when he wears that tattered shirt
I don't really mind at all.
It represents the things he learned
That helped him grow so tall.

SANTA'S SECOND SLEIGH

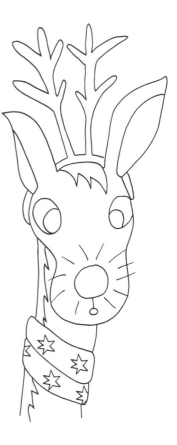

It's good to have a backup
So Santa bought a second sleigh
But could not afford more reindeer.
(They eat too much hay.)
Instead he bought nine llamas!
Yes, one has a crimson nose,
And when he calls them all by name
This is how is goes:

"On Dolly and Molly!
Light it up now, Bahama!
Let's keep it punctual,
Period and Comma!
Not while we're flying,
Please Spitter and Phlegm!
Someone tighten the antlers
On Kissa and Tim!

I'm really impressed with how much you can carry
But I'll switch to alpacas if you get too contrary!
Llamas cost less and they don't mind the snow!
Except for those contracts I'd have switched long ago!
Have you forgotten a gift for your mom?
Then buy a toy llama on Santa dot com!
They're cute and they're fluffy and have antlers as well
And unlike the real ones they hardly do smell!
So on to the rooftops with Bahama in lead!
You'll get extra presents 'cause I'll spend less in feed!
The reindeer don't mind! They're resting a spell
Which by tomorrow I'll be doing as well.
And when you get presents from under the tree
Remember it's thanks to the llamas and me!"

THE ADVENTURES OF BILLY THE BROWNIE

He stands at fourteen inches, tall as brownies go,
And his feet are big and flat so he can walk on snow.
He watches all the kids in our neighborhood
And sends a fax to Santa who's naughty and who's good.
His ears are long and pointed and he hears more than an elf
And I would not believe this save Bill told me it himself!
It was Christmas Eve and lights had not been strung.
I went to grab a stocking. At least they would be hung!
And inside was Billy Brownie, resting fast asleep!
He must have had some eggnog else he wouldn't snore so deep.
He woke up with a start and moved to get away
But the twinkle in my eye must have said it was okay.
His voice was kind of squeaky, sort of like a mouse,
And he told me he would help me decorate the house.
You should have seen him move! He was quicker that a cat
And the tree was all decked out in just two minutes flat!
I offered him some chocolate and politely he agreed
And told me 'bout the time our kitten had been treed.
"I'm supposed to watch for Santa but that's one thing that I missed
And it took me seven years to get off the naughty list!"

I asked him, "Why the secrets?
Why do brownies stay in hiding?"
But he sadly shook his head,
"I'd get in trouble for confiding.
We work really hard
Right through Christmas Eve
And the smiles on Christmas morning
Are the presents we receive."
I nodded slowly, wondering,
If what he said was true
And, if I were a brownie,
What things I might do.
Perhaps a gift or favor
To help someone in need
And never let them know
Who had done the deed.
I looked up at the star
That Billy placed so high
And when I looked down he was gone
In the blink of just one eye.
Quick and nigh invisible
And caught so very rarely,
The brownies want us all
To treat each other fairly
On Christmas Day and every
Other day as well.
That's why Billy talked with me,
As near as I can tell.
But brownies are a funny sort!
They like their secrecy
So let us keep this personal
Between just you and me.

ONE DOGGONE CHRISTMAS

Brutus is our rottweiler, a delightful breed, you know.
He changed the course of Christmas about five years ago.
He liked to chase the mailmen back into the street.
I've seen them leap the six foot fence! (For some, that's quite a feat.)
We didn't have a chimney so Santa came that way.
Brutus thought he was a mailman who had come to play.
For Brutus is quite color blind. (He can't tell red from blue.)
The brownies gave no warning so Santa had no clue.
I've never seen a fat man run so fast as he
And we were sad to find no presents underneath the tree.
But Brutus had a patch of cloth in his gaping jaws
And at noon we got an e-mail signed by Santa Claus.
"You'll have to get a ladder. Your gifts are on the roof.
I've left the seat of my old pants with your rottweiler as proof.
I can't bring them all inside. (This job is too demanding.)
Once I met your rottweiler I spent the whole night standing.

The brownies won't go near him! They're afraid they might get chewed
So we'll have to ask your neighbors if you've been bad or rude.
No system can be perfect but we'll do our best, you know.
You can take delivery on the roof or tossed out in the snow.
Don't even think of suing. (My attorney can beat yours.)
Besides, I have as evidence my tattered pair of drawers."
He closed his short epistle with "Merry Christmas, Friend!"
And, like indoor delivery, our story's at an end,
Except for one brief message my son sent in reply,
"At least I know the reason I saw two moons up in the sky!"

MY ROLLER SKATES

I like to ride my roller skates
'Cause I can go so fast.
Just ask the nice policeman
Whose patrol car I just passed!

MY ROLLER SKATES

I love to ride my roller skates!
They take me everywhere.
I've never been to jail before
But now I'm going there!

FOUR OUT OF FIVE DENTISTS AGREE

Four out of five dentists all say
That I should put my candy away,
That I should brush each morning and night!
Vertical strokes or it's just not right.
Your gums will recede if you do not floss.
They talk to me as if each one were my boss!
Who thought that teeth could give someone such thrills?
Four of five dentists love using their drills!
Cavities take them on cruises and trips
And I think they like numbing my tongue and my lips!
I sit in the chair and tremble in fear
When four of five dentists are gathering near.
Whatever else happens they always agree
And the person who suffers turns out to be me!
I won't go to the dentist's! They can't take me alive!
(Unless and of course you've found number five.)

WHY PHYLLIS BURNED THE BARN

She calmly led the horses out.
The cows and pigs were next
But why she left the hay inside
Left us all perplexed.
She said it was intentional
Which we couldn't understand.
How could such a perfect girl
Behave so out of hand?
They asked her at the station
And she told them straight away
It was because she had heard
Snakes were in the hay.
Now we all have our blind spots
And idiosyncrasies
But if there's a snake inside our house
Could you just TELL me, please?

NICKLE, PENNY, DOLLAR, DIME

Nickle, penny, dollar, dime!
I'd take you all if I had time.
I'd take you with me everywhere,
To the park and to the fair,
To entertain my lady so.
Come on, fellas! Won't you go?
Here she is! Ain't she sweet?
I'll buy her just one little treat:
A ring to put her finger through!
What's that she says? That won't do?
She needs a car, a house, and maybe
A crib and playset for – a baby?
Dollar, dime, nickle, penny,
I'm married now and haven't any!

COOKIES BY A ZOMBIE

The words were very strange.
I paused and shook my head.
Why would someone bake a cookie
If he or she were dead?
Digestion wouldn't work
And you surely couldn't taste!
I wonder that a Zombie
Would have such time to waste.
So I had a conversation
With the Zombie down the street
Who told me that a cookie
Was more than just to eat.
"It really is an art," it said,
"Like baking poetry,"
But when I read my poem
Here's what it said to me:
"As a Zombie I am dead
But still I am no dummy
And your poem's like a cookie
Because it's very crumby!"

STANDING ON BOXES

I'm standing on boxes
On top of a chair
Two hundred feet
High up in the air!
And I ponder this question
In my altitude rare,
"Do you have a parachute
Or a ladder to spare?"

THE FATTED CALF

I went to hunt the buffalo
Across the fruited plains
So you would not have to eat
Refrigerate remains.
I saw many buffalo,
A thousand maybe more,
But I couldn't figure out
What this bow and arrow's for!
I stalked rabbits and beavers and ground hogs,
Squirrels, dove, and deer,
But my hunting skills have failed me!
I have none, I fear.
I'm afraid that I may never
Slay the fatted calf
But I brought home a pizza
And you can have a half.

BUTTERFLY WINGS

A poem is a moment
caught like a butterfly.
You have to let it land
for you'll hurt it
if you try
to catch it in a net
or
trap it in a jar.
Words apart so common
now brought together
are
so fragile
and so beautiful
like a butterfly's new wing
and from cocoons
placed in my mind
I love to watch them spring.

WARRIOR IN THE LAND OF KINGS

I'm a warrior in the land of kings
But I won't kneel and kiss their rings
For I'm the one the people follow,
A fact that kings find hard to swallow.
And though besieged on every side
I would rather fight than hide.
For I know that victory's mine
If not in these realms, those divine!
For a warrior rules not by decrees
But through the souls his battle frees.
The warrior fears not for his fate.
His courage is what makes him great.
And when the final trumpet's blown
I'll be upon the highest throne
For in the end one truth remains:
In the land of kings, the warrior reigns!

Inspired by comments by Dave Guckes
and in tribute to my father, Dr. Dale von Rosenberg,
a warrior to his final breath
whose spirit lives stronger now more than ever

COURAGE IS ITS OWN REWARD

Toil and trouble, fear and pain,
Can I stand when powers wane?
With this answer my mind fills:
"Courage dared always instills
An attitude of 'Yes! Can do!'
That human spirit does renew.
A habit stronger, now restored,
Courage is its own reward!"

Do I quit or do I stick
When the battle's going thick?
And failing first is it I
Who then will give a second try?
Better, stronger, once again,
Determination full to win
As through the fray I sound this chord:
Courage is its own reward.

I look up to the mountain peak
For it's such goals I constant seek.
Weary yet no pause to rest
For there is joy in such a test.
To my limit, stretching past,
Exhilaration! Here at last!
Whatever goal I'm aiming toward,
Courage is its own reward!

What, to me, do these words mean?
A different outlook I have seen!
Ends and outcomes change for me
When with courageous eyes I see.
The path through life steep and rough
Yet heart of courage is enough
To serve as both my shield and sword.
Courage is its own reward.

All do strive for earthly gain
But in the end just these remain:
Honor, courage, faith and love!
For such ideals rise far above
All the things to have and hold.
Oh, for courage to be bold
To measure these as life is scored.
Courage is its own reward.

SEVEN HORSES

Seven horses by the fence
Leaning over for some hay,
One horse does the opposite
And turns the other way.
Seven horses nodding
As though to give applause,
One horse flicks its tail!
Does it know my flaws?
Seven horses looking up
As I stroll along
But from its stance there's one horse
That says I've got it wrong.
I strive for perfection
And unanimity
But am grateful for this one strange horse
Because it humbles me.

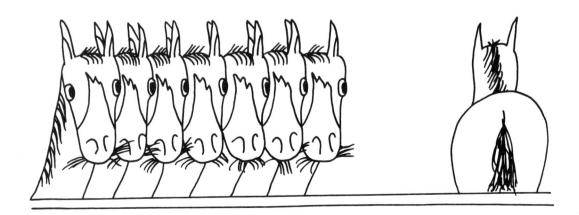

MY TEACHER'S
UNDERPANTS

When I was at the store downtown
I happened, just by chance,
To see my teacher buy (on sale!)
A dozen underpants.
Some were checkered, some were plaid,
Some were polka-dotted,
And it seemed to me that twelve is more
Than teachers are allotted.
I never thought that teachers
Gave thought to underwear,
Much less that they would decorate
Their bu- -! Excuse me, derriere.
Oh, that I could wipe away
Those thoughts deep in my mind
Like what is in between
My teacher's trousers and behind!
It wrecks my concentration!
My grades are falling so
And I've decided that's one thing

I JUST DON'T WANT TO KNOW!

SPOT, THE TALKING BUG

I thought I'd left the TV on
But the noise came from the rug
Where I made acquaintance first
With Spot, the talking bug.
I picked him up and held him
In the palm of my right hand
As he proceeded to regale me
With discourse glib and grand.
At first the softest whisper,
His voice began to boom
Moving my emotions
And sending tremors through the room.
He made me laugh! He made me cry!
Such vision he portrayed
Inspiring me to action,
A man and bug crusade!
I was in his hand
As he was deep in mine
And I rose up to my feet
To hear his last opine.
Yet so impassioned was I,
My manners I forgot
And clapped my hands together –
How rude! Sorry, Spot!

MY BUTLER

He wakes up at the break of dawn
And starts his daily chores,
Tiptoes very quietly
And softly closes doors.
He gets the paper, takes out trash,
Turns the TV on
And starts a load of dishes –
All this before it's dawn!
He feeds the dogs. He feeds the cats.
He cleans the kitty litter
But he says he's going to quit
If we get another critter!
He drives my daughter to her school
And goes to get our mail.
He shovels snow in wintertime,
The driveway without fail!
He mows the grass in summer
And rakes up leaves in fall.
Without my butler I don't know
If the house would stand at all!
My wife thinks that it's great
Since my butler works for free
But I don't like it half as much
Since my butler's me!

MY HOT TUB

I loved to use my hot tub
But then the heater died.
My mama said, "Don't do it!"
But stubbornly I tried.
I used it through the winter
And I watched the water freeze.
Now I'm asking Mr. Groundhog
If he would kindly please
Not see his scary shadow
As the dawn's warm rays are felt
'Cause I'd like to have an early spring
So I can finally melt!

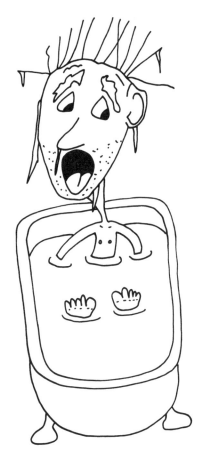

WASHING SOCKS

I never have clean clothes
But the washer's always on.
It's been three whole weeks
Since my last sock was gone!
I went and asked my wife
Who's using all the water.
She said to solve the mystery
I should ask my daughter.
My daughter said each set of clothes
Must be washed upon its own
Depending on the color
And the kind of cloth that's sewn.
"There's some time next Tuesday,
In the morning, two o'clock.
You'll have a half an hour
In which to wash a sock.
And maybe Friday afternoon
You can do a second one.
You'll have to leave work early
If you're to have that done."
I shook my head in solemn
And complete defeat
And took my clothes in baskets
To the cleaner's down the street!

WHY, OH WHY?

My teacher says she's busy.
She has much too much to do
And no time for herself
When all her grading's through.
She has cooking and cleaning,
Resting and reading
And grading this test
Takes the time she is needing
To contemplate and celebrate
Her life and simply live it
Which makes me wonder this:
Why did the woman give it?

UNCLE ALFRED'S EARS

My Uncle Alfred was very strange.
Of that, there is no doubt.
He could raise his eyebrows one at a time
And wiggle his ears all about.
People came from miles around
When Alfred was just a mere lad
And told his parents how lucky they were
And what a talent he had.
Uncle Alfred took it all in,
The spotlight, glory and fame,
And though he was never quite normal
He was able his pride to keep tame.
"I never did nothing to earn it,"
He told me one day on his stoop,
"For talent is kind of like ice cream.
It's good! Every flavor your scoop.
Yours might be vanilla or chocolate.
I might prefer peppermint.
Use all your talents for good
And enjoy them for they're heaven sent!"
With that he wiggled his ears
And gave me a wink and a nod
And I think of him often and well
Even though he was, frankly, quite odd.

NOVOCAINE

He numbs my brain with Novocaine
But my dentist is the worst.
He gave me seven shots for pain
But did the drilling first!

THE GINGERBREAD MAN GIVES A HAIRCUT

The gingerbread man has half a head
But he's a cookie so he's not dead.
He got a job at the barbershop
And gave my hair his special chop.
Without his eyes he cannot see.
Look at what he did to me!
So please, I beg you! Don't go there!
Just get your Mom to cut your hair.

NEANDERTHAL NED

Neanderthal Ned had a club in one hand
And in the other he held a gold wedding band.
He came up behind Nell to tap her soft head
But she twisted around and here's what she said.
"You'd better learn manners, you big bellied brute!
Shave! Lose some weight! Wear a tie and a suit!
Learn how to read, you big hairy dope,
And take a good bath! This time use the soap!"
Ned gave her the ring and went down to one knee.
The result of this meeting's now quite clear to me.
I'm bathing at home and learning at work
And changing the diapers! Am I a big jerk!
It's not now enough to bring home the bread.
I have to be sensitive! Thanks a lot, Ned!

CAVE MAN DIP   SOAP

THANK YOU CANDLE CHARM

They have lily of the valley
And perfume of the rose.
Candle Charm has scents
To cheer up every nose!
Get one as a present
To help a friend get well
Or give someone a hint
About a better way to smell.
I finally got the message.
(I have one beneath each arm!)
And my wife and all my friends say,
"Thank you, Candle Charm!"

A PITCHER OF ELEPHANTS

"Take a pitcher of the elephants!"
My daughter said to me
But the one I have's not big enough
As you can plainly see.
Yet my little joke was not lost
On my teenage son
Who got a pitcher big enough
So I could fit in one!

THE RIGHT TOOTHBRUSH

When it's time to brush
What are you going to do?
What color do you like,
Yellow, red, or blue?
This one has hard bristles
That exercise your gums
But that one has the softer ones
That dig out all the crumbs.
This one changes colors
To tell you when you're done
While that one sings a song
To make your brushing fun.
Oval heads and square ones,
Rectangular and round,
Everywhere I look
Another one is found!
So many kinds of toothbrush
In my bathroom - eight or nine! -
Which leaves me with a question:
Which one of them is mine?

EARTHWORMS II

I ventured out one fine spring day
In the merry month of May.
I picked an earthworm off the street
And tossed it on the grassy peat.
The earthworm wriggled, twirled around
And tried to dig into the ground.
Sliding under damp moist bark
That worm was hidden in the dark.
But its fortune wasn't very good.
A robin landed on that wood!
I tried to make it fly in fright
But the worm was gone in just one bite.
My neighbor saw me running there
Trying to give that bird a scare.
"Were you trying to save that worm?"
"I was!" I said, standing firm.
He said, "That is kooky and absurd!
I'd gladly feed them to a bird."

My neighbor's wife was on a walk
And clearly heard our happy talk.
She knelt in her garden to do some work,
Started to dig, then turned with a jerk.
"Honey," she said, "Here's what I read:
Earthworms are good for our flower bed.
Go to the street and pick up a few.
You wouldn't mind,

WOULD YOU?"

My neighbor mumbled so I barely could hear
But he blushed bright red as he said,

"Yes dear."

MELALEUCA MELANIE

She wrestled a gator as big as King Kong!
It was twenty feet high and two hundred feet long!
Crossing the Outback from Sydney to Perth,
They flattened the mountains right into the earth.
Over and back and into the sea
Where the gator cried "Uncle!" and she let it go free!
The crowd clamored, "How? Tell us, Mel, please!"
Mel calmly replied, "It's in the oil of the trees.
When I was a girl I had root bark to lick
So I grew up real strong and never got sick.
It's been part of my day since I was quite little
And look at me now! I'm as fit as a fiddle!
Stronger than cannon, tank, or bazooka
Is the oil of the bark of the tree melaleuca!"

She was fearless and never gave heed to the "can'ts"
Like she heard on a trip to the shoreline of France.
She was going to England from the town of Calais
But the seas were too rough for the ferry that day.
"Let someone else ride," she said. "I'm going to swim it!"
"No, Mel!" they begged. "It's way past your limit!"
But she covered her body in the oil of that tree,
Took a big gulp and dived into the sea!
She never arrived at the white cliffs of Dover
And the legend of Mel was thought to be over.
But seven days later the world woke to a shock
When she arrived in New York and climbed up on the dock!
She had leaves and bark to eat as a snack,
Then Mel the Mighty dived in and swam back!
She lived a life of adventure and fun
And as far as I know Mel always won!
And I think it was more than the bark that she chewed.
It was the strength of her character and how it stayed glued
In spite of disaster and challenge and fate.
Mel always believed she could carry that weight.
She conquered her fears and learned to excel.
In your journey through life, may you do as well!

THE POET LAUREATE OF BYRNES MILL

I want to be the laureate
of the Village of Byrnes Mill,
A position I will take
Since there's no one else who will.
I'll regale you with my stories
And astound you with my rhymes.
I've asked if you would hire me
About a hundred times.
I'll take the job for nothing
And give you twice as much.
Think how good our town would be
With my poetic touch!
And now the drum roll starts!
It's voting time again.
The mayor went home sick
So this time I might win.
He argued and he hollered
Until his face turned blue
But now I'm poet laureate
By a vote of three to two!

THE PYTHON POEM

I'm trying to use a python
To squeeze out a poem today
As I've been having some trouble
Thinking of what I should say.
And now that my blood pressure's rising
I'm seeing stars and hearing a roar.
I'm on the verge of writing a sonnet
So I say to the python, " Squeeze more!"
Yes! This really is working!
Of that there's hardly a doubt.
Now quick! Hand me a pencil and paper
So I can write it before I pass out!

A COMPLAINT FROM THE MAN IN THE MOON

Hey, neighbor! What did I do to you?
What's with the cow? This ain't no zoo!
And why did you send me a fork and a spoon?
You're not coming to dinner 'til you change your tune.
Oh, I know the songs. I hear them crooning
But everyone knows what it means to be "mooning"!
I've always been the light in your sky
But you shoot rockets at me! And I ask you, why?
What did I do to make you so mad?
We were the only neighbors the other one had.
But now you have satellites buzzing and soaring.
Yeah, I get TV and the programs are boring.
You've become quite a nuisance, a bothersome pest,
So it's hard for me to get any rest.
But I won't be moving for try as you may
I'm the Man in the Moon and I'm here to stay!

A WHOLE NEW TURN

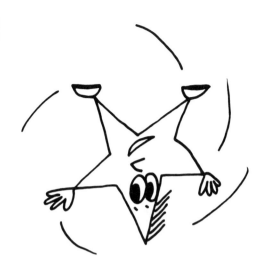

Oh, the twists and turns of fate
That mark us either poor or great!
Do events we don't control
Consign us to a certain role?
Or are we somehow greater than
A pawn in someone's cosmic plan?
Do I quit or do I try
When my ventures go awry?
For should I one more time begin
'Twill be a stronger go therein,
One to change the distant stars,
A better future to be ours!
With grand affairs I will contend
To see them to a different end
For when I strive the things I learn
Give my life a whole new turn.

OF COLANDERS AND CALENDARS

I thought about the difference
Between these disparate things
As I met the New Year
With the musing that time brings.
I pondered on the colander,
How most things pass right through
And realized that with calendars
That's what happens, too.
Which things are important?
What items will I keep?
With colander and calendar
I pluck them from the deep!
And look at how they shine
And sparkle in the light,
The gems of truth and knowledge,
So precious in my sight!

ALL THE TEA IN CHINA

All the tea in China!
All the cats in Siam!
The gold in ol' Fort Knox!
That's how in love I am.
I used to think that I could be
In love – oh, just a little! –
But now I've lept the fence
Without stopping in the middle.
It's a whole new attitude
That's inside me now
And the police say I feel better
Than the local laws allow.
It's all because of you,
Your smile, your laugh, your touch!
And because you told me
You love me twice as much!
For all the cats in Siam
And all of China's tea
Don't mean half as half as much
As does your love for me!

SHARE A DREAM

Have a seat
beside me
as the sun begins to set
and we'll talk
of things to be
that haven't happened
yet.
The outcome of your dreams
that are so brave
and bold
and of mine
that are the same
though
I have grown quite old.
You have life
ahead of you
much more
than do I
but the dreams
I have are beautiful
just like
 the evening sky.
They are in need
of younger hands
that will live
to great the morn
for only in
another's heart
can they be
reborn.

If you can see
the beauty
in the moon's
soft beams
then take them through
the night
to the morning
of
your dreams!
Let the dream of freedom,
beauty, honor,
peace,
be the guiding force
that gives your life
increase.
And when
the sun has set
no longer
think of me
but of the dreams
we shared
and how
the world should be.

OLD SCHOOL

I wonder at the darkened stairs,
The cracks and pealing paint.
The school I used to think so new
Today seems rather quaint.
The halls where I once roamed,
The teachers I once knew,
All seem somewhat worse for wear
Yet I am older, too.
And the questions I once asked here
That I thought had gone for naught
Were answered in the lessons
That outside these walls, life's taught.
And so it's safe now to return
For what have I to fear?
The sticker that I wear
Says I just visit here.
Looking back, I should have worn
Such a sticker every day
To remind that life, like days at school,
Does surely slip away.
And so the gray-haired gentleman
Walks out the door again,
Smiles and wishes all the best
For the students walking in.

SEAGULL FOR A DAY

If I could be a seagull but only for a day
I wouldn't work at all. I'd just fly around and play.
I'd catch the ocean breezes and soar into the sky,
Thankful that for just one day I had wings to fly!
I'd scan the far horizon and try to bring it near.
Maybe I would rather be seagull for a year!
But that's enough of dreaming. I have work to do right now.
Seagull for a minute is all that they allow.
And yet we went together on a little ride
So part of me will always be a seagull deep inside.
Yes, seagull for a minute in this body I call me
Is sufficient for my spirit to live forever free!

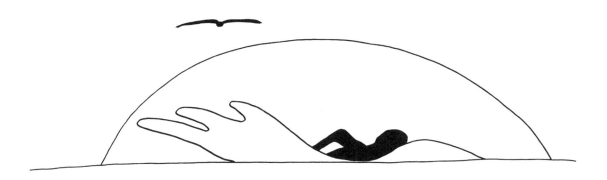

SPIRIT AND MEMORY

I've been told
I write a lot
about the nasty
bills I've got.
People think
it's way too much
and that I have
the Midas touch.
Sure! I might
sell you a book
but what about
the loans I took
to help us go
when we were sad
or cure us of
the ills we had?
Not to mention
printing cost
and how last year
we almost lost
our house, our home,
our wedding rings
yet we would sacrifice
these things
to tell a poem
here to you
and watch you smile
when I got through.
For what is life
if not the grace
to give up what
we can replace
for things that live
eternally
in spirit and
in memory?

LIGHT BLUE ALPACAS

Light blue alpacas
Are happy, it seems,
Or that's what they told me
Last night in my dreams.
They fly in a flock
Or is it a herd?
When I say it out loud
It sounds so absurd!
But I think of alpacas
And llamas a lot
Which makes people wonder
If I'm crazy or not.
"Imagination," I say,
"Is a wonderful thing
From whence light blue alpacas
Suddenly spring."
But my doctor says should
They return for a visit
He's bringing a net.
Hey!
That's not for me,

IS IT?

After a visit from the Light Blue Alpacas
In the "I Don't Want to Kiss a Llama!" Store

78

OVER AND OVER

You say that we must fight
And one of us must lose
But there are other options
That I would rather chose.
For I have come to realize
The price we each will pay
And so ask you one more time
If there's not another way
Since both of us must lose
For one of us to win,
A lesson man forgets
Over and over again.

TOO MUCH TO HANDLE

The bank that charged me late fees, thousands by the minute,
Had to close its doors! There was no money in it.
The one that turned me down for too low a credit score
Was shut down by the fed and they're not open anymore.
The card that charged percentages higher than my age
Had its CEO locked up in a cage.
And I wonder how it is that I with income mediocre
Am being asked to pay to re-employ my broker.
I'm told that we all need them. They really know their trade!
So how is it they didn't save a dime from what they made?

What'd they do with all that money?
Was it just too much to handle?

Unfettered greed has always
And will always lead to scandal.

AS IS

Dining room chairs in the basement,
Boxes of books in the hall!
The dishwasher's making some noises
But it's not cleaning at all.
The cats and the dogs just keep shedding!
Their hair's on the carpet like snow.
There are only twenty-four hours
Then the realtor's coming to show.
The grass has to be cut.
The walls need to be painted.
When my wife went to clean up the bathroom
She opened the door and just fainted!
Yet tomorrow it has to be sparkling
And looking exactly like new
So if you'd take it just as it is

I'd probably give it to you!

EIGHTEEN DOCTORS

I talked to eighteen doctors
seeking their advice
and each one recommended
I visit at least twice.
And so I changed my schedule,
saw a doctor every day!
You should have seen the bills
that I had to pay!
But I'm sure that it was worth it
for each doctor was degreed
and it would have been an easy choice
had any two agreed.
"Surgery!" "Holistic!"
"Medication." "Wait!"
"Take another test.
I must evaluate!"
Eighteen different doctors
and thirty-six opinions
not including nurses,
orderlies and minions.
So the choice is up to me
and I don't know a lick
except this bit of wisdom:

"YOU'D BETTER NOT GET SICK!!!!"

Dr. Quak

THE EAGLE AND THE DUCK

The eagle and the duck
Each know how to fly
But a duck can also swim
While the eagle must stay dry.
A duck can do this naturally
Without questioning the why
But an eagle wasn't meant to swim
And, apparently, neither was I.

THE MOST MONUMENTAL POEM
THAT EVER WAS

A ballad of epic proportions!
A hero of wisdom and might!
A plot with exotic contortions,
A monumental poem to write!
Phrases a fragrant as flowers
And as smooth as the finest of wine.
Fame, fortune, and powers,
Imagination to make all these mine!
Tastes like the sweetest of honey!
Shines like the brightest of gold!
Swim in an ocean of money
As millions of copies are sold!
Perfect in rhythm and rhyming,
The most monumental poem that was!
Exquisite in its timing
Yet it's also tragic because
This poem of the ages,
This quintessential book,
Is not found within these pages . . .

My editor gave it the hook!

84

ADAM'S ATOMS

Molecules always move about
And Adam's atoms, too, no doubt.
So don't be surprised if he should leap
Even though he's fast asleep!

And if he should rise so high and far
To meet up with a shooting star
I hope he'll wake up just a bit
So he might perhaps remember it!

ALFRED THE ELF

Alfred the Elf loved mathematics,
Cerebral things and thought acrobatics.
Not making toys but equations instead
He solved lots of problems right there in his head.
His parents and friends said, "Alfred! Enough!
Elves weren't made for numbers and stuff.
No one takes elves like you seriously!
Why must you ponder so ponderously?"
But Alfred stuck with his quotients and numbers
For there is no telling why anyone hungers
For things that seem difficult in another one's view.
Hey! We don't have to explain the things that we do!
So hold on to your dreams like Alfred the Elf
And you'll bring out the best of what's inside of yourself.

GOLDILOCKS FROG

Goldie Frog broke protocol and took a brazen dare,
Waited 'til the bears left home and ate some porridge there.
When the bears returned they said they'd call the cops
But Goldie Frog said she'd heat some more to make them lick their chops.
"Not too hot!" said Poppa Bear. "The stuff will burn my lip."
But Goldie Frog just laughed when he spat out his first sip.
"I can cool mine down," she said, "with a little puff of air,
Something you can't do 'cause you're just a stupid bear!"
Her counsel that the bears should wait and let the porridge thicken
Abruptly ended with the words, "Mmmmm! Tastes like chicken!"

Goldie Frog! Oh, Goldie Frog!
The porridge was too hot
But lucky for the bears,

THE REST OF YOU WAS NOT!

BLINDERS ON HORSES

They put blinders on horses
To restrict what they see
But horses don't wear them
When they're running free.
And I wonder what I'd do
Or what I might be
If I could take off the blinders
That they've put on me.

ADVICE FROM
MY AUNT WINNIE

The advice from my Aunt Winnie
When my ears were turning red
Was clear, concise, and firm:
"Put that cap back on your head!"
But it wasn't only practical.
She was kind and wise
And the words she said could often
Take you by surprise.
There was the time I lost
My very favorite toy
And she knew just what to say
To help that little boy.
"I've looked everywhere," I said,
"That it could ever be!"
"Then look somewhere it couldn't!"
And her words helped me to see
Not only just the toy I found
But other things as well:
Ideas, dreams and meaning
In the stories I now tell.
"Dare to think and dare to dream
And seek out your own way!"
Advice from my Aunt Winnie
I've followed to this day.

OUT OF

Out of sorrow, happiness.
Out of sickness, health.
Broke one minute then the next
Dabbling in wealth.
Life can turn in many ways,
In good not just the bad
And today is always different
From the yesterday you had.
Can you make it better?
You can always try
So face life with a smile
And for once don't wonder why.
Gather all that's good
In the golden light.
Relax and breathe for everything
Is going to be alright.

IVAN THE TERRIER'S CHRISTMAS

He's not concerned with presents beneath the Christmas tree
Although the chance to shred them fills his eyes with glee.
But it is really more than something he can chew.
For Ivan this thing "Christmas" is those special things we do.
I can see it in his eyes as they snap open wide.
"Christmas" is a chance to chase the ball outside!
To him it doesn't matter. It can be any date.
A little bit of time and Ivan thinks it's great!
For him it is Thanksgiving, New Year's and Christmas Day
Any time and every time I say the words, "Let's play!"
And I wonder as I throw the ball into the fading light
If the dog that chases it has somehow got it right.

THE MAN WHO LIVED IN A WELL

I once knew a man who lived in a well.
How long he'd been there, nobody could tell.
He seemed to be happy with nary a care
And I thought he was lucky to be living down there.
Until finally one day he gave a great shout,
"Hey! Somebody up there! Please help me get out!
I want to see sun! I want to see sky!
And though I may fail, I just have to try!
I'm cold and alone. I'm lonesome and scared.
I've never known love from someone who cared.
Throw me a rope, a ladder or net
And I'll be your friend! I will not forget!"
So I threw him a rope and he climbed to the light
And never complained that the sun was too bright
Or the rain was too cold or the wind was too strong,
The summer too short or the winter too long.
So when I feel like my life's at a stop
I think of that man when he got to the top
And my heart fills with thanks more than I can tell
Because of the man who lived in a well.

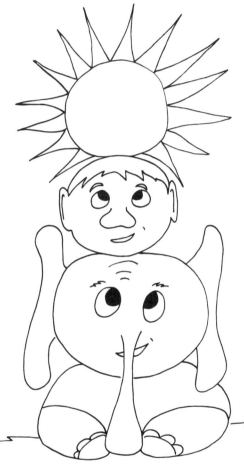

WHAT THE ELEPHANT FORGOT

It forgot its great big ears
Might make some people laugh.
It forgot it wasn't skinny
And tall like a giraffe.
It forgot that it was strange
To have a trunk shaped like a hose
So it forgot to chuckle
When it looked at your big nose.
But it remembered sunrise
That opened up this day
And it remembered happiness
That's found in work and play.
It remembered power,
How strong that it can be,
And all those things together
Somehow reminded me
That elephants and people
Can travel very far
When they forget their differences
And remember who they are.

WHISKERS ON SEALS

Whiskers on seals would tickle as much
As those on my cat but seals' I don't touch.
But I'm scratching the ones on my very own chin.
Whiskers on seals have me thinking again.
In so many ways we're alike, you and me,
But you're too far to reach like the seals in the sea.
Yet thoughts can reach farther than whiskers e'er could
To tickle the mind and share what is good.
So I hope you can sense these good feelings I feel
When you look at the whiskers on the face of a seal.

PENNIES IN A FOUNTAIN

Pennies in a fountain tossed so long ago,
Wishes from a little child – Like me, did they grow?
Did I set a course with each tiny wish?
For a penny in a fountain is more than food for fish.
It is a feast for thought and though specifics fade
I am living out the wishes that little child once made.
Thoughts lead one to action so choose, and choose them well!
Will your wish come true? You, and time, will tell.

ALL ABOUT ESTER

I know all about Ester
Who drinks too much caffeine.
It turns her from "just cranky"
Into downright mean!
She snaps her fingers, waves her hand
And hollers really loud,
Embarrassing the waitress
And upsetting all the crowd.
One time I stopped to talk with her
Before she came unglued
And found she didn't really mean
To be so doggone rude.
It was her medication
And she couldn't sleep at night
And she says that she'll be better
Once they get it right.
I sure do hope that's true
'Cause I can no longer bear it
And next time she yells for coffee

ESTER'S GOING TO WEAR IT!

CAMP CURE

I just found a tick on my pants.
The lunch that I brought is covered with ants.
Chiggers and fleas are making me scratch
And my ankles are red like an apple or match.
Spiders and bedbugs live in my sheet!
Camp is where nature - those bugs! - and I meet.
So I twitch through the night and rise with the dawn.
The bugs seem to like the sprays I put on.
I got bit by a snake and finned by a fish.
I asked to go camping and I got my wish.
I spent thirteen days in a bunk with a mouse
But tomorrow camp's over! I'll be back at the house.
It's been nigh a month since I've had a shower
So let's hope there's hot water enough for an hour.
For I've fought and I've battled and, yes, I've endured
But as for this camping . . .

Don't worry!

I'm cured!

TWO MORE FIDDLES

With two more fiddles I might find a string for one right note
Or strike upon a melody as good as any goat.
I could simulate the sound of squeaking brakes.
(Two would do it better but one is all it takes.)
I could get an innocent to admit to crimes galore
As long as I would promise not to fiddle anymore.
Music has a power given by the gods
But harmony and fiddles are constantly at odds.
I tried to teach a thousand applicants to play.
I failed! But with a fiddle it doesn't matter anyway!
Beneath the harvest moon I fiddled through the night.
That's what made the cow jump over it in fright!
With two more fiddles I could start a music revolution
And if you want me not to play you'll make a contribution.
You'd better dig down deep and find a lot to give
'Cause I've got two more fiddles . . .

98

... AND I KNOW WHERE YOU LIVE!

THERE'S AN OUTHOUSE IN BYRNES MILL

On the top of a hill here in Byrnes Mill
An ancient outhouse stands
Where you can sit and look beyond
To many far off lands.
To India and China,
To Nome and Timbuktu,
People's thoughts go wandering
And I find that mine do too.
But as I peer into the vastness
Of those skies away out yonder
My contemplation's personal
For it's closer things I ponder.
Indeed the pressing question,
The one thing I must know
E'er I leave this rustic throne is,

"Where'd the paper go?"

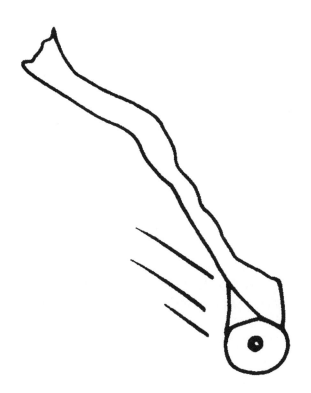

WOBBLING WILLIE WOODARD

It's a wonder Willie Woodard never came to fame
Though it's only through coincidence that we now know his name.
He was quite an acrobat, the best in his whole town,
And he walked upon his hands to see things upside down.
But there were lots of people who did not understand.
They shuffled feet and kicked to stir up dust and sand.
Willie sneezed and shook his head to recover from the shock
Then sought the higher ground and climbed the steeple clock.
They came from every house and farm for many miles around
Calling up to Willie, "Get back down on the ground!"
And Willie, when he saw them there chose that time to speak.
"Listen loud and clear," he said, "before you call me freak!
The things I say and do seem to be so strange
But I propose that each of us might need to make a change.
Show some understanding to different folks like me
And if you can't do that, perhaps just let them be.
Try to be a friend and they might be one back
And help you on some distant day when you're under like attack.
Together we might build a better world and town
And since we can't all fit up here I'll be coming down."
With that he tumbled nimbly back onto his feet.
Quickly he descended and joined the crowd there on the street.
And that's the last we've heard of wobble-walking Will
But the words he spoke that day give us guidance still.

DETERMINATION DEEP

Today I met a statue
That looked just like my son
And wondered of the life he led
And all the things he'd done.
And though he could not speak
And tell me what he knew
He made me pause a moment
To try the other shoe.
So young and full of confidence
To seek his wealth and fame
Like me so many years ago
And my son who does the same.
Did he have an inkling
Of the perils that befell?
The past much like the future
Hides and does not tell.
Yet in that face and in those eyes
There is determination deep,
A look that says that I have found
A single dream to keep.
What mystery is this
That his face appears again?
Yet so it is with all the dreams
Deep in the heart of men.

WHEN THE LAST CLOUD'S PAST

What happens when the last cloud's past
To reveal the bright full moon?
Does it portend clear skies ahead
Or a new storm coming soon?
When will the last wave hit the beach
And the ocean's pounding cease?
Will there ever be a time
When all on earth know peace?
Who will be the person
To think one last thought of hate?
Can you change your way of thinking
Or is it much too late?
For as the waves bear down again
And press on waiting sands
You have the answer to that question
Right there in your hands.
Now that the final cloud is past
What will the heavens do?
Look inside your heart and mind
For that depends on you.

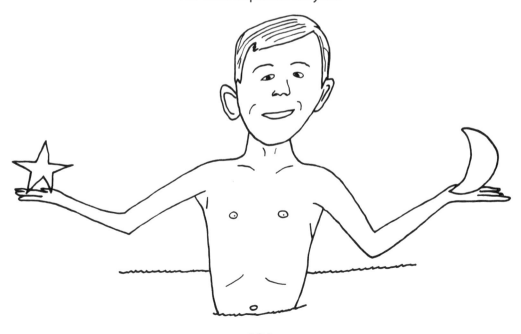

104

ELBOWS AND KNEES

I have a pair each of elbows and knees
That help me to balance and stand as I please.
There's a part of my mind that helps them adjust.
It's not as much thinking as learning to trust.
And so I can walk. I can run and I play.
With my knees and my elbows I'm finding my way.

They're not very pretty.
(I scrape them a lot.)
But I've come to accept
They're the best that I've got.

And I wonder if also there is deep in my mind
Something that helps me when I'm caught in a bind.

Determination and courage

For me are those keys
That keep me in balance like elbows and knees.
A gift and a choice, they're a part of me, too.
In difficult times they help me get through.
And though I can't see them like elbows and knees

There is nothing more vital
In life than are these.

A QUIET MAGIC

There is a quiet magic all about this place
that slows the hands of time to a peaceful pace.
I feel it in the air, the sweet and gentle breeze,
that whispers soft this message,

"Relax. Do as you please."

And I am not the only one who has fallen in its spell
for I see the smiles of children and older folks as well.
So many things have changed but this place is still the same,
unaffected and untouched by any worldly game.
The quiet magic grows for it is deep and strong
with a melody more beautiful than any heard in song,

joyous as the sunshine
that falls in rainbow bands
and thick enough to catch
and hold it in our hands.

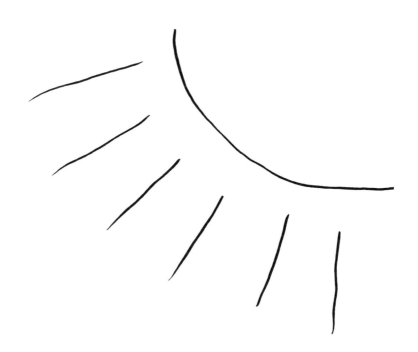

SLOW NOTION

I lie upon the beach
Free from any motion
Listening to the seagulls
Fly above the ocean.
And as I start to rise
I get a sudden notion:
Before I went to sleep
I should have used the lotion!

RED OR GREEN

I think they all were color blind on this morning's drive to work.
One guy stopped when the light was green!

I almost hit the jerk!

And as I made my final turn it happened once again
And gave me cause to wonder what universe I'm in.
I stopped a traffic cop as he was passing by,
Told him what I'd witnessed so he could tell me why.
He shrugged his shoulders, then he sighed
And resignedly he said,

"Why not stop on green?"

"They already go on red!"

BENJAMIN FRANKLIN FROG

Franklin-Frog behaved
Well outside the norm
Flying kites on a hill
In a thunderstorm!
He wanted to be known
As a somewhat greener Ben
And prove that frogs could be as good
In science as are men.
The lightening flashed! A cloud of smoke
Rose up from the field
As an elemental principle
Of physics was revealed.
Lightening often strikes
The highest point of land
So anyone with any sense
Will find somewhere else to stand.
What makes a frog or person
Think he is exempt
And treat a common truth
With loathing and contempt?

Franklin-Frog! Oh, Franklin-Frog!
Was it smart to fly that kite?
Well, there was that one brief moment
When you were pretty bright!

PEANUT BUTTER PETE
DOESN'T HORSE AROUND

Pete thought he'd have a little go at the local rodeo.
Picked a bronco strong and lean, hungry, too, and kinda mean.
It threw all the 'pokes who tried but Pete was sure that he could ride.
Said Pete, " I know just what to do! I'll use my PBJ as glue!"
But he didn't let the PB set, a fact that he would soon regret.
The bronco bucked when Pete sat down, threw Pete and saddle back to town.
Pete heard its loud and angry neigh. Said, "That horse could use some PBJ!"

He wired the PB factory for information just to see
If he could order peanut butter by the trough or in a gutter
So he could feed it to his horse and make a friend of it, of course.
It came by train just two days later and Pete got dressed up as a waiter,
Grabbed the bronco's reins and led it to the PB trough and fed it.
The horse's eyes snapped open wide! That PBJ felt good inside!
Pete rode it through the pasture green, the gentlest horse you've ever seen.
With PB in its oats and trough it didn't try to throw Pete off.
Pete knows he'll never lose his grip and he is always quick to quip
"When you make a peanut butter friend they'll stick with you 'til the end.
Crunchy or smooth, with jelly or jam, peanut butter is who I am."
I like it, too, so I must say, "Join me for some PBJ!"

THE RAIN DANCE

They danced all day and through the night
In hopes the clouds would grow and might
Break the drought that for so long had cursed their native land
Never giving up through they could barely stand.
They kept their frantic pace through evening number seven
When the distant thunder announced a gift from heaven.
With energy renewed they left it not to chance
And everyone rushed out to celebrate in dance.
It rained three days and nights and all the lakes were filled
And everyone who danced that day had this thought instilled:

Faith must be persistent to show the greatest gains
And a rain dance only works when you dance until it rains.

THE TURTLE CROSSING

I called the mayor to discuss the city's turtle care.

"You should study them to know the why and where
They cross the road so they wouldn't get run down!
We need a turtle crossing right here in our town!"

The mayor put his head in his trembling hands.

"But where?" he asked. "That's what no one understands!
For even topnotch experts are at a total loss
Since there's never been a turtle that got all the way across!"

THE WEATHERMAN POEM

He predicted cold. It was hot.
He said it would rain. It did not.
He looked at the radar and saw a big blot
And said a tornado would form in that spot.
"Hide in the basement! Crouch in the hall!"
But the blot was a bug out for a crawl.
The people were grateful for they had been spared
And gave thanks to the weatherman for how they had fared.
They bought him a dinner and gave him a plaque
"After all, it's the weather! Let's cut him some slack!"
He told us the reasons he didn't get sacked
And made no excuse for the sense that he lacked.
"I look good with the lady who anchors the news.
I have a nice voice and hit all of my cues.
Now some of you think I'm not very bright
But remember that somewhere, I'm always right."

THE WISEST OF CATS

The wisest of cats
Slept under some hats
That were laid on the bed for a party
And I later said
She'd have stayed off of the bed
If she really were such a smarty!

FEEDING THE GOATS

Goats to the right and goats to the left
Bumping and nibbling me!
Eating my laces, socks and my pants
From the ankle right up to the knee!
And now I look like a beggar
Or a bum in raggedy clothes
And it's all because of the goats
That my shoes are revealing my toes.
I hear people mumble and murmur
As they watch me trudge down the street
While others give me a dollar
And tell me, "Get something to eat."
My mother is shaking her head.
My friends all say it's a shame
And I've been summoned to court
To determine who's really to blame.
Meanwhile I'm taking donations
Of leftover shirts, pants and coats
So I can go back to the farm
And spend the day feeding the goats!

GEORGE WASHINGTON FROG

They say that little Georgie Frog
When he was just a 'pole
Got an axe and set his sights
On the tree atop the knoll.
And though he was quite tiny
He chipped and chipped away
And he was over halfway through
When he heard his father say,
"Georgie Frog! Who has been
Chopping down this tree?
It's best to tell the truth
So do not lie to me!"
And Georgie Frog with ax in hand
And set atop his heart
Told his father solemnly,
"In this I had no part."
Suddenly the tree gave way
With a loud and awful "POP!"
Landing on poor Georgie Frog
Whose lies came to a stop.

Georgie Frog! Oh, Georgie Frog!
Woe is woe is you!
You're flatter than a pancake!
At least that part is true.

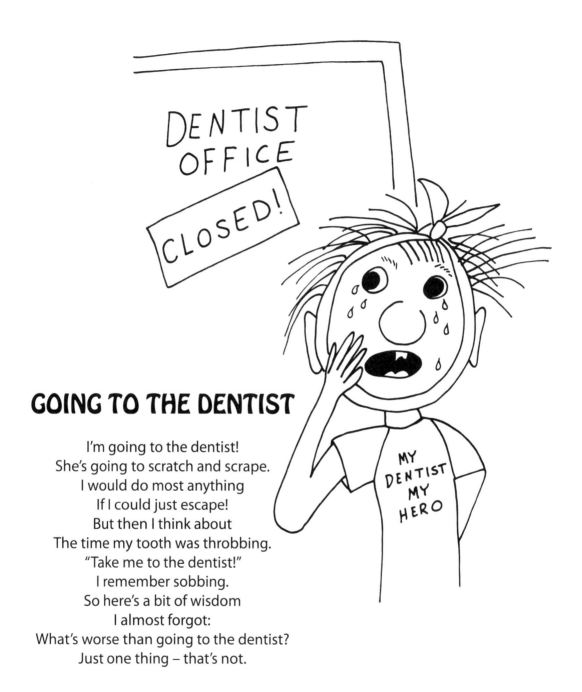

GOING TO THE DENTIST

I'm going to the dentist!
She's going to scratch and scrape.
I would do most anything
If I could just escape!
But then I think about
The time my tooth was throbbing.
"Take me to the dentist!"
I remember sobbing.
So here's a bit of wisdom
I almost forgot:
What's worse than going to the dentist?
Just one thing – that's not.

THE BEST AT STINKY

I chased a skunk into the woods
and much to my dismay
it welcomed me not with a kiss
but instead its awful spray!
I know not why it felt a call
to have such a bad reaction.
For fourteen days I have bathed
yet still reek its olfaction!
Tomato juice don't cut it!
Don't think I didn't try.
They tell me I'd smell better
if I'd just up and die!
But I think I've learned a lesson
that I'll pass on to you:
There are some things in this life
It's better not to do.
Don't sniff your brother's shoes!
Don't pull your grandpa's pinky!
And don't mess around with skunks
'cause they're the best at stinky!

THE ZEBRA AND THE PEACOCK

Despite its stripes a zebra
Doesn't see in black and white
And it contemplates the peacock
With all its colors bright.
And when the peacock peeks
At the zebra's back
It might like the elegance
Of plain ol' white and black.
It's in the beholder's eye,
The beauty that we see,
A fact that I am grateful for
When you look at me!

LITTLE BITTY LEPRECHAUNS

Little bitty leprechauns
Stole my gold away
So it's not my fault these bills of mine
Are impossible to pay.
I went out with a gnome last night
So he could be my buddy.
He made me flunk my math exam
'Cause I forgot to study.
I think it was a unicorn
That poked me in the eye
So if I crash my car today
That will be the reason why.
I didn't start the fight!
The ogre must have done it!
If the brownies hadn't held me back
I know I would have won it!
And if it wasn't one of them
It probably was the elf!
The only one who's not to blame
Is I and me, myself!

MILTON THE PIRATE

Milton the Pirate had longs locks and a beard.
With a hook and an eyepatch he looked pretty weird.
He had tattoos on his arms, his legs and his nose
And on his behind but I haven't seen those!
He had rings in his ears and gold covered teeth
And a bone-handled sword in a crocodile sheath.
The sea where he swam was pretty polluted
Which made his hair frazzled and his mind convoluted.
He had one wooden leg and scars on his chest
But Milton looked better than all of the rest
Of the pirates who also set sail
Leaving their women to scream, cry and wail
For it could be years 'til they return from the sea
And so in the meantime, will you go out with me?

I WANT TO BE A PIRATE

I want to be a pirate! 'Tis my fantasy
So I went to Captain Hook who was the man to see.
He had an eye of glass and a hook for his left hand.
He wore a wooden leg and a scar made by a brand.
"Aarg!"
He said with half a tongue and just one tooth left in his head.
"You'd be a lucky lad
To live the life I've led!
I've sailed the seven seas
And all the oceans wide.
Yes, I've lost a limb or two
But I still have my pride."
But I think he paid too high a price in search of earthly plunder
And as for you who read these words, will you do the same, I wonder?

PSYCHIC KIM

This is the story of Psychic Kim
Who told people what would happen to them.
It seems that Kim was always right
Which more often than not gave them a fright.
She told a neighbor he'd fall from a tree,
Break an arm and skin a knee.
Another would lose his job today.
They came for his car and took it away.
They formed a mob (Kim predicted that)
And she got out of town in two minutes flat.
She saw the danger she put herself in
And predicted she'd NEVER do that again.
She still tells her stories like she used to do
But she predicts NONE will ever come true.
I suppose it's sad she was too good at prediction
But she makes more people smile with fables and fiction.

124

TRY TO LISTEN

The birds and stars all speak to me
And I hear the zephyrs blow
As if all of nature's children
Want to tell me what they know.
I've even tried to listen
To people as they speak,
Not just on TV
But the common and the meek.
It helps me to find truth
As I walk my way through life
But I'm constantly in trouble
'Cause I still can't hear my wife!

EATING OKRA

Blackened, grilled,
Sauteed real hot,
Boiled for hours –
Looks like snot!
Nothing seems
To hide the taste!
Grocery dollars
Gone to waste!
Over roaring campfires
Hanging on a stick,
Okra never fails!
It always
Makes me sick!
"Hide the taste!" I thought
And had it batter fried.
There's not a single thing
That I haven't tried.
I went to ask my Grandma
Just the other day,
"How should you eat okra?"
There had to be a way.
She looked through all her cookbooks
Trying to recall
But I liked Grandpa's answer:

"JUST ONE WAY. THAT'S NOT AT ALL!"

BUTTONS FROM THE SKY

In the closet depths I found my favorite suit
And a nice silk shirt! A leather belt to boot.
I was going on a business trip and packed them all away
And saved them for a meeting with my boss today.
I tried it on this morning. It had a tighter fit
And I had to be real careful when it was time to sit.
My boss gave us a speech. It was his best, I think,
But as dinner settled in my suit began to shrink.
It was not the words but the suit that made me cry
And I think it was the sobbing that brought the buttons from the sky.
And with the raining buttons laughter also fell
And the story is a favorite my office likes to tell.
And if there is a moral to this sad, sad tale of woe
It's to try on all your traveling clothes just before you go.

MISSING AT THE WEDDING

Call the caterer for cake!
Order up some punch
And those little sandwiches!
Say we need a bunch.
Get flowers for the table,
A bouquet for the bride
And find some extra chairs
To get everyone inside.
An organist, a soloist,
We've got to have a pastor!
And don't forget the cameraman!
That would be disaster.
But everything is perfect now.
Everyone's arrived.
The wedding's almost ready
And I think I have survived.
I can smell the flowers,
The roses all in bloom.
There's only one thing missing.

I'll go get the groom.

LEMONADE

Lemonade
in the shade
with the summer breezes blowing.
Nice and cool,
A swimming pool
Down my throat now flowing.
Summertime
I think that I'm
Getting hot again.
In fact I figure
If my glass were bigger
I'd be jumping in!

MUDDY SHOES

Muddy shoes are bad, I know,
Evidence of melting snow
And yet the little one who trods
Calculates not the odds
Of judgment from a steely frown
As he ambles hallways down
To wake his mother with a kiss
And share with her a secret, this:
A flower from the garden grown,
The seeds of spring finally shown,
And joy enough in such great news
To surely pardon muddy shoes.

THE BIGGEST VINE

Bigger than the beanstalk
Of Jack and giant fame!
Taller than the redwoods
That Californians claim.
Denser than the jungle
Where Tarzan used to swing!
Blacking out the sun and moon
So I can't see a thing.
The EPA declared it
A vegetation zone
And says it can't be tampered with
Because of how it's grown.
The record book says it is
"The world's most gigantic vine!"
That ever grew on any house –
I just wish it wasn't mine!

SOGGY BUNS

I went into a restaurant
To have a simple meal
Surprised to find inside my box
Something awful to reveal.
No, it wasn't something living
Or thin catsup as it runs
But the worst of all encounters:
Hamburgers with soggy buns!
I couldn't even pick it up
Without my hand becoming wet
And when I told the manager
He said something I'll ne'er forget.
"Sir, we carefully craft each meal.
We're well aware of what's inside!
We've always had these soggy buns
And we serve each one with pride!
I have soggy buns
Each and every place I go.
I like my soggy buns
And so does everyone I know!"
I was completely speechless
And did not know what to do
For I like my buns firm and dry
And I think my wife does too!

132

BYRON FROG

He started to write verses
Of the rhyming kind
And it seemed to all his friends
The frog had lost his mind.
He couldn't get it published.
It was lousy, more or less,
So he took out all his savings
And bought a printing press.
The frog knew how to write
But he didn't like to read
So he didn't get instruction
Like novices all need.
The press ate all his paper
And still kept stamping out.
The frog dived in to stop it
But no one heard his shout.
It sold a million copies
But he's not there to sign
Though they say that you can see him
In the print that's really fine.

Byron Frog! Oh, Byron Frog!
Your prose is heaven sent
And we're glad to see your face again
Though it's flatter here in print.

THE FALLEN WAVE

Towering it loomed, cresting towards the sun.
Foaming! Falling forcefully towards the sand, then done.
Lapping – oh so quietly – at castles made of sand
Seems a bitter ending for a wave that stood so grand.
And yet the water rushes back to build another giant
For the ocean does not long remain docile and compliant.
The fallen wave has life again, is constantly renewed
As are youthful dreams that failure once subdued.
There is a tempest brewing far, far out at sea
And dreams that are much stronger that yet give life to me.

There is rises! Now it falls.
Yet ever, always, my dream calls.

NAMING THE RABBITS

Twenty-two rabbits with cottontail rears,
Eighty-eight paws and forty-four ears!
The children can call each rabbit by name
But to my adult eyes they all look the same.
It's a matter of time I guess and suppose
To find something special in the touch of a nose,
The blink of an eye or the turn of a head.
There are too many things I'm watching instead
Like deadlines and schedules and bills overdue,
Things that a child called me never knew.
And thinking of this I realize again
That life can be simple for me like back then.
But slowing down life takes changing some habits
So I'm watching the children and naming the rabbits.

THE NINTH PIG

She started out behind,
The smallest of the litter.
It would have been quite easy
To grow up mad and bitter.
But she never gave up trying
And always found a way
And the ninth pig of the litter
Has won first prize today.
Something happens deep inside
When someone does their best
As though through disadvantage
We are sometimes blessed.
No one can imagine
How someone else may grow
In the daily turbulence
Of mortal to and fro.
It took the smallest pig
To help me realize
That success does not depend alone
On brawn or brains or size.
It depends on attitude
That just will not give in
To overcome the obstacles
And have a chance to win.

ESCUCHEN!

According to my Spanish class
Which I was fortunate to pass
"Escuchen" means to listen well
But there was about a ten year spell
Beginning in my middle teens
When I had not tendency nor means
To "escuchen" much in any tongue,
Indeed to use both lip and lung
To persuade folks to my point of view
As no one knew the things I knew.
And though people sometimes say I've changed
It's really just how I've arranged
My words in rhythm and in rhyme.
I'm still the same for all this time!
For I believe that good will win,
That when you fail to try again,
That love's the world's most potent force
And honesty's the clearest course,
That faith and hope and deepest trust
In the end will win and must
And though my voice is softer now
And there are wrinkles in my brow
The conviction that a young man held
Holds as firm as any weld.
For all the trials I've ever known
My certainty has only grown
So call me stubborn if you will:
This is what I stand for still.

AL, THE BANNISTER BOY

He'd gotten scrapes and bruises from his falls and trips
And earned a blackened eye, some scars and swollen lips.
But Al was quite the acrobat at his home and school
And he liked to slide on banisters against the local rule.
They were fixing up the courthouse with some paint and plaster.
The banister looked shiny and he thought he could go faster.
But it had been a decade since the doggoned thing was sanded
Which Al discovered quite some time before he even landed.
It took his mom an hour to pull out all the splinters
And he hasn't slid on banisters for nigh on thirty winters.
Alan learned a lesson that's hard for girls and boys:
Things that aren't made for it should not be used as toys!
"But it looks like so much fun!" That's what they always say
Until they figure out how much they'll have to pay.

MY MAGIC CARPET

It looked kind of like Aladdin's with its Persian weave
And the power was much more than I could e'er believe.
It would spin and hover when I gave a tassel tug
And take me to the moon! It was a special rug.
It took me south in winter and to the beach in spring
And I was quite astonished to be owner of the thing.
I thought that I should give it perhaps to a museum.
Yesterday I called the board and sauntered down to see 'em.
They accepted in an instant and I went home to get it
But my wife had thrown it out

Because the puppy wet it!

"Woe is me!" I cried as I bowed my doleful head
Whereupon my wife remarked,

"And the kitty wet the bed."

Now I can't bequeath my carpet but there's something I can do:
I'm going to take the dog and cat

And give them to the zoo!

ONE TOO MANY

We went out to the county fair to see a man called "Snake"
Who let those serpents climb on him for hours with no break.
I did my best to count them. It was a hundred, pretty nigh,
But Mr. Snake complained, "There's something gone awry!
We'd better get to looking 'cause I think that one is missing!"
And suddenly my mother's purse moved and started hissing!
She screamed and threw it up and it opened in the air
And the snake that slithered out landed in her hair!
There are certain pitches that humans cannot hear
And I'm lucky that I only lost the hearing in one ear.
If they were keeping records how far a snake was hurled
I think my mother would be known as champion of the world!
But she's not one to brag. She won't talk about it any
Except to say that as for snakes,

"ONE IS ONE TOO MANY!"

MY UNIQUE PHYSIQUE

Hercules and Atlas!
Such names do come to mind.
"Hippopotamus!" says my wife
With one look at my behind.
But one thing I can say
Is that I am quite unique
Since there's no one out there trying
To copy my physique!

THE HAT COLLECTOR

Meet the hat collector who lives in our upstairs
And amazes all his friends with the different tops he wears:
A baseball cap for every team, both big and minor leagues,
Sailor's hats and army caps, both dress and for fatigues.
He has a dozen crowns and many more berets,
A different hat to wear for at least a thousand days.
He can change our moods as a jester or a clown
And he always draws attention when he goes into town.
Sometimes it is positive and others it is not
But there are times you have to show off what you've got!
And though he collects some ridicule with his compliments

Being who you are
Always makes good sense.

THE COMMON
TRIBULATIONS

We are not above
the common tribulations
that confront, confuse
and trouble our relations.
Often it's the little things
that start with just a trickle
yet add up to remind us
how life can be so fickle.
High atop the mountain
and in the moment next
frustrated, angry
and, most of all, perplexed
at how the tumble happened
– Oh! – so very quickly
and life that seemed so smooth
has somehow gotten prickly.
For no matter how you think
life has made you wise
the common tribulations
will catch you by surprise.
And then it's time to take
a step back from the fray,
reflect and reevaluate
and go about your day
and hopefully take with you
a whole new set of mind
that leaves your tribulations
and troubles far behind.

AN ACT OF TRUE KINDNESS

An act of true kindness
Is an incredible sight
For taking the wrong
And making it right.
Give someone who's hungry
A piece of your bread
And you'll find that your spirit
Also is fed.
Give someone who's weak
A strong hand to hold
And look for the same
Should you dare to grow old.
Some people need time.
Try spending a while
Sharing a story,
A laugh or a smile.

Kindness is never
One way like a street.
Without it no person
Is ever complete.
Isn't there someone
You can help out today?
If you think just a moment
You might find a way.
Reach out with your thoughts,
Your heart and your mind
To try to bring forward
Those left far behind.
Try it today
As never before
Then go out tomorrow
And do even more.

MISSING ME

I've been missing me.
I've been gone a lot
doing many things
I would rather not.
But I have to pay the bills.
I have a part to play
and that must be the reason
I've been missing me today.
Other people "know"
who I'm supposed to be
so they never think
I might be missing me.
But now I stole a moment
to visit me once more
so I feel a good bit better
than I did before.
And I wonder if I met
someone else who did the same
I might get to know them
past a face and name.
And wouldn't it be wonderful
and wouldn't it be swell
if I let them know me
in that same way as well?

145

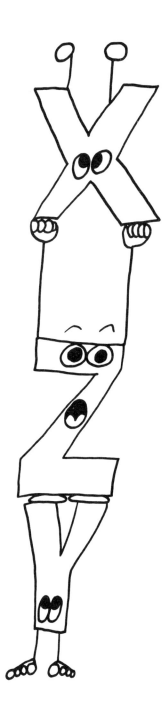

X AND Y AND Z

I wonder what the reason is
For X and Y and Z.
Do we really need them?
It's not so clear to me.
X could be replaced
By C and K and S.
We might be better off
If we had one letter less.
Now Y is simply silly,
Both consonant and vowel!
Why the newest of our readers
Might just throw in the towel!
Z has no defenders
Except the chimpanzee
So let's call it something else!
That would be fine with me.
Ecksept I am not sure
How this looks to ewe.
Without these letters I'm afraid
Life might be, well, a zoo!
Not everything is logical
And it's a good thing that it's not
So let's keep X and Y and Z
'Cause I like them a lot!

SNAKE SKINS AND LOCUST SHELLS

Reminders that they once were little
There they lie, broken and brittle.
Once a shelter lived inside
The living part has split it wide.
In its new skin the snake has grown
And slithered off to parts unknown.
The locust grew and left as well
And what remains is just this shell.
That seems to be the way life goes.
Something's lost as something grows.
The locust and the snake have gone
And as I grow, I too, move on.

AUTHOR'S NOTES

I've been a bit bored today so it seems like a good time to write up these Author's Notes. I've already eaten a candy bar and some chips and if I don't do something I won't be able to fit in the picture on the next book! That's what happens if you're not VERY careful when you reach your 40's and 50's and yes, you too will get there someday. But don't think about that now. You've just gotten this book and you're wondering if it's going to be worth your time to read it. Well, I can't speak for this part (because I haven't written it yet and it's out of my genre - isn't that a great word?) but I do think you will enjoy many of the poems in **Stars to Chase**. It's been about four years in the making but a poem book is just a collection of the poems I like best. I made a table of contents about 18 months ago and it's been changing ever since. Hopefully I've put the best ones in! I do hope you get a smile from it.

Before I get into writing about the various poems and how I came up with the titles, I thought I might answer a question I get asked a lot at signings. It's about publishing a book and how to get yours done. Unfortunately I don't have an easy answer. I'm still self-published after selling over 25,000 books so I may not be the best person to ask. Nevertheless, here's a bit about my experience and I hope it's entertaining if not helpful.

I started writing poems regularly when my dad was ill with Lou Gehrig's disease in 2002. I wrote a poem for him and it touched many members of my family. My wife Sharon and I looked up how to copyright things on the GOVERNMENT website (there are a lot of them that are NOT official government websites so make sure you get to the right one) and sent the poem in. We later found out that your poem, story, song, or novel is copyrighted as soon as you write it. You don't need to send it in anywhere, but I send my poems and drawings in about once a year just to be sure. It only costs about $50 or $60 and goes to the Library of Congress.

We attended a conference early in my writing career and ended up self-publishing my books. That can be very expensive and you have to buy a lot of books at one time, although now you can get them in smaller batches with the on demand publishers. We didn't do that because we were trying to get into bookstores and distributors and on demand was not returnable at that time. Big box bookstores will not take your book if it's not returnable.

I finally got a big box bookstore to let me do a signing for a teachers' appreciation night about 4 months after it came out. They were very helpful and found a local book distributor to carry my book, which meant I got 45% of retail for sales instead of the 35% I was getting from the distributor arranged by my publisher. You have to figure the retail price of your book based on making at least a little from such sales, and then make retail or wholesale sales if you are to make it financially. But signings are great to do anyway, because you meet so many neat people and that can lead you to a presentation at a school, church or civic club where you can sell your books at retail. That's when it starts to pay off a bit more.

We had seen some authors at Silver Dollar City in Branson so we tried to get in there. They referred us to a store in town where we did well. I watched the other authors and read books on how to market at the point of sale. We gave away free chocolate llama kisses (just chocolate kisses) and bookmarks. Later we held drawings for a stuffed toy llama. For a couple of years we maintained a book of addresses, phone numbers, and emails, but those did not lead to the sales we expected. We eventually decided to change to children's books (my first two books are inspirational poetry) because people really like pictures with their poems. We chose to do hardcover because of how they feel to the customer. And we cut out an extra middleman so we could keep the price where we wanted it. *I Don't Want to Kiss a Llama!* is in its sixth printing and has sold over 13,000 copies in less than five years.

Things change a lot in this business and I guess you can't get too sentimental about it. We used to go to Branson fifteen or twenty times a year and now we go much less often. Fortunately we've been able to develop places closer to home that like having me there. I try to make sure no one feels pressured to buy a book. My job is to make people smile. If they give me their time knowing I want to sell them a book, then I'm the one who has been given a gift so I respect and treasure it. Sometimes they do come back and buy and it's always great when someone crosses the mall to say how much they like your book.

We now have our own store called "I Don't Want to Kiss a Llama!" so I haven't been selling at the big box stores much because other places give me wholesale and allow me to visit whenever I want. Big box bookstores will generally only let you in once a year or so. That's not enough to make it on your own.

I have been on TV three times in the seven years I've been doing this. I did get on radio a lot for a time, but that's harder and harder as they consolidate programming. Not many stations have that local program and a lot of people want to be on. I do have a website at idontwanttokissallama.com and have gotten my signings in the newspaper quite a bit in the past. Again, they keep changing the ways to get listed, so it's hard to keep up.

There are a lot of books out there telling you about the ISBN numbers you'll need, Books in Print, contacting the big book stores and the technical things you need to get your book done. Like I said, those things change so quickly that I think you're better off getting a recently published book about that.

What I will tell you is to expect to be challenged on a daily basis. There are many gatekeepers and they know how to guard their turf. Look for the open gates and go there. But just remember, a dream is only yours if you recognize it and fight for it BEFORE it becomes apparent to everyone else. I lost a dream once because my family was threatened. I made a very difficult choice and spent years trying to revive that lost dream. Writing children's books is a dream I will not give up. Read *Dale the Uniclyde* or "Ivan the Terrier", "Leading the Unicorn", "Endgame" or "Turnabout Mountain" from *Thinking Upside Down* for more on dreams. When I read them, it deepens my resolve. When I read *I Don't Want to Kiss a Llama!* it makes me feel better!

Was that boring? Sorry! Go back and read your favorite poem if this is making you drowsy. Now to the poems and how I came to write them.

"The Bed Sheet Parachute" is one of my favorite poems because it's a true story that was told to me by an elderly gentleman from Oklahoma. I had recited "Walter Wupperman's Wings" and he said,

"That reminds me of the time I jumped out of the tree with a bed sheet parachute!" I put in the rhymes but the story is pretty much as he told it to me.

"Shakespeare Frog" took many tries before I hit the right formula. I kept trying to make the poem revolve around some of the more obscure plays until I finally realized it had to be **Romeo and Juliet** and the balcony scene at that. I've now written a dozen or more "famous flat frog" poems and maybe I'll make that into a book or a calendar sometime. Some of them will have to go into **The Hidden Things**, which will be my next book of poems.

I have a love/hate relationship with "Goldilocks Frog". I think the poem is very funny, but it is kind of mean. I was just writing some more famous frog poems and that one seemed like it was worth working on.

"Byron Frog" is NOT about me. It's inspired by the famous English poet, Lord Byron whose name was something else entirely. But seriously, who remembers that?

Notice that "George Washington Frog" has a tail as well as is a tale. That's because he's a tadpole so I guess I misnamed the poem but, hey, it's my book! Write your own and you can do the chapter titles yourself if you want to. Really, you should write a book or a journal or a poem because there's something someday that only you will see, a connection only you will make, and a truth only you will discover. If you don't write it down, it will be lost forever.

Did I just try to make you feel guilty? Sorry! Write because it's fun when you discover yourself and the world around you and you can do that by writing. Really, you can!

"Juan Pablo Madrid" is a poem inspired by a friend of mine from camp many years ago. I almost typed "fiend of mine" and JP was a bit devilish about some things. I remember when he tried to take his canoe down the South Fork of the Caney River in Tennessee right into some impassable rocks. He would have been killed, but he shrugged it off. "Too easy!" is what he said when we stood above the falls and looked down at the site of his almost demise. JP and his brother Andres came to camp with us one summer not knowing much English since they were from Mexico City. Wow! They sure made camp interesting! Andres told us that JP passed away a few years ago, and that got me thinking and writing. You would have liked JP I am sure.

People often ask me to write a scary poem for them. Well, what could be scarier than "Old Cheese"? My wife really thinks that I eat old cheese and leftovers too many days after they've been opened, but I have been secretly reading the expiration dates and not telling her. Do something once and it will haunt you for a long time! She went out of town this morning and threw away all the old cheese and anything else that was going to expire before she got back!

"No TV" is pretty scary. I guess "No Computer" or "No Cell Phone" would have been scarier to most of you readers of the younger generation. Wonder what it will be for the generation that follows you, when all your electronics are passé.

Did you notice all the dentist poems? I don't mind the dentist so much but my wife really doesn't like going. When she finally has to go, it's usually because something hurts. I prefer going more often. I don't like them digging too deeply in my mouth. And I really can't stand it if my teeth hurt. Did you know babies should go to the dentist? Parents need to know how to care for the baby's teeth before they are old enough to do so or some pretty bad things can happen. Sharon, Ryan and I found out the hard way. Learn from our experience, please!

Do you like looking at the clouds and finding the animals? That's how I got to write "The Pig and the Poodle." It's funny, but clouds also inspired "When the Last Cloud's Past" which was first printed in my book, **Climb the Red Mountain**. I used to watch the sky more but now I usually just watch the dog when I take her out to pee. No plans to write about that but you're welcome to the idea if you want. As for the pigs, they do better in "The Pig Has Wings" which gives me perspective on how fortunate I am to have been born when and where I was born. There are things a very common and not very wealthy person like me has done that would have made kings jealous a hundred years ago.

And the pigs also do better in "The Ninth Pig" which was inspired by a visit to my mother's house last year. One of her neighbors had eight decorative concrete pigs set out in her yard. For some reason I was counting them (Did I tell you I graduated with a degree in Chemical Engineering which requires a great deal of math?) and then noticed a ninth pig hidden in the bushes. I love finding an interesting title because it so often leads to an interesting poem and a bit of truth, which is what poetry is all about.

I suggest that you don't impose your will or your own ideas on a poem. That's what "Butterfly Wings" is about and it is how the poem came to me. I had to stop the car and write because the poem was unfolding in my mind and I was afraid it would fly away before I could stop. The ideas are already there in the creative part of your mind. Poetry is merely a way (not the only way) to let them out.

There are a lot of people who want to impose their will on you. Read "Sharks to Chase" or "Too Much to Handle" to give you an idea of what I mean. That's as close as I come to writing about political things. Not too much truth to discover in that field, I'm afraid, and I admire the people who do battle in that arena who are able to stick to their principles. Actually, it's tough to stick to your principles in any field. The reward is worth it, like "Melaleuca Melanie" found out and as illustrated in "Our Eagle". We got family from all over the country to come to celebrate my son's award and accomplishment. I hope your family has many such things to celebrate and enjoy about one another.

There are a few camping poems again. I never thought I'd get tired of camping when I was a young man, but I rather like my house and my bed these days. I do remember how camping and adventure helped me grow up as you can see in "Therein Was the Dawn" which was originally written about a camp somewhere in New Mexico. "Camp Cure" is much more like I view camping now. I love the out of doors, but I like to go home at night. And I like bugs less and less.

Maybe that's what makes poetry so much fun these days. It contrasts the attitude I held as a young man with the perspective I've acquired through the years. I'll write about that some more in **The Hidden Things** with a poem I call " Youth for Wisdom". Meanwhile in this book you can read about that transition in poems like "Buttons from the Sky" and "Snake Skins and Locust Shells". I got inspired for the buttons poem by talking about the suit I was wearing on the set of the movie

Up in the Air which was filmed in St. Louis. I was an extra but I am in the movie! (I am the blob on the upper left who waves for a cab at the very end of the movie when George is deciding where to go with all his airline miles.) I told my daughter Erin that "I'm a movie star and you're not!" and she just shook her head and said, "You're weird and I'm not." The price of fame, I suppose.

Okay, here's a bit of seriousness. Don't worry, I won't spend too long on it. You may know that my poetry started with a prayer for my dad called "Look at My Hands" which I wrote as he was dying of Lou Gehrig's disease. He faced his fate with an awesome courage, which I cannot imagine myself ever doing. But his example leads me to do things I would also never do and show courage I would never before have imagined. I mean, if he can face that, surely I can face the financial difficulties of publishing and promoting my books in an effort to bring a smile or a bit of truth to someone else. Courage truly is its own reward, and life IS the grace to give up what we can replace for things that live eternally in spirit and in memory. One small step often leads to many larger and more daring ones. End of sermon except to say that my Aunt Winnie gave me great advice without preaching it and that's a skill only a few special people have. And until I wrote the poem "Advice from My Aunt Winnie" I didn't even know that she was advising me. And if you could ask her today, she'd probably tell you that I'd have figured it out on my own anyway. I'm glad she was there for me.

Aunt Winnie had absolutely NO relationship with my Great Uncle Alfred of the wiggling ears and maniacal eyebrows. Uncle Alfred was one of those unique people who would be called weird if they had no money, and eccentric if they had a lot. I don't know about Uncle Alfred's finances, so I'll just say he was quite memorable.

"Two More Fiddles" came from a joke someone told me in Branson one day. I started writing about two more fiddles and what I could do with them. I didn't know how I was going to end it but when I got there, the last two lines were there for me. I love it when that happens!

Branson is a pretty place and so is Jefferson County, Missouri near St. Louis where I live. I wrote a bit about the town I live in, Byrnes Mill, in this book. No, I am not and have never been the poet laureate of Byrnes Mill (or anywhere else for that matter) but I did go to a city council meeting and ask them for the job. Never heard a thing! The mayor quit shortly thereafter and I wonder if I was the cause!

There IS an outhouse in Byrnes Mill and it is near the top of the hill where I often jog. You can't see it in the summertime because of the trees, but it has probably been there 70 or 80 years at least. No, I've never used it. I have found it best to "go" before I "go" on my travels about the neighborhood. Read the poem and you'll know why!

My family and I have come to love it here in Missouri after moving so much as a young family. I am putting the following poem in the Author's Notes because it is personal and expresses my feelings about the state. I hope you understand, and have similar feelings about the place you live.

HEART OF A NATION

Deep within her bosom the heart of a nation beats
From country roads and rivers to the noise of city streets.
From her wheat filled plains to the paddies of the 'heel
Missouri is America where dreams transform to real.
From the hills and hollows we can hear her song,
Beautiful and boisterous! Humble, and yet strong!
Nations rise and flourish from the vigor in their hearts
And America is blessed that Missouri's where it starts.
It flows as mighty rivers from this blessed land
Endowing me as well for Missouri's where I stand!
Here I'll make my home where my own heart has found
A wholesomeness of spirit in Missouri's hallowed ground.

Willie Woodard was a real person and lived in New England somewhere back in the early 1820's
I think. I read about his escapades in a book somewhere but it was just a line or two. See what
happens when you let your mind run wild? Maybe I'm the weird kind of person Willie was talking
about! Could it have been you? (No, you don't have to answer that. These are just my silly thoughts
to take up a few pages of this book and make it long enough for you to do a book report on it.
Come to think of it, several students have used poems from this book to recite for poetry month in
April, and you are certainly welcome to do that. Have fun!)

Yes, of course I had to put Neanderthal Nell on the back of the book again. I suppose she's not
the prettiest gal I could use, but I don't have to pay her any royalties since she's not a real person
and would be dead several thousand years if she were. Did you notice I wrote a poem about her
husband, Ned? We are each influenced by the lives of those who have gone before, and we will
influence the lives of the ones who follow. So try to do a good job of it, 'kay?

There was a young man at one of the schools where I was talking, and he asked me if I was rich.
Don't I wish? He wanted to know if I had a butler, so I thought a moment and said, "Yes, I do. You
are looking at him."

"You're not rich," he said.

Not in money, perhaps, but I feel rich whenever I write something that has a bit of truth in it or
makes someone smile. Just wish it paid more at the bank at the end of the month when we have
bills to pay!

Look and listen. Write and see what happens. A friend of mine was complaining about the
"eighteen doctors" she had to go to, and how one of them didn't like her decision to go ahead with
surgery without getting even more opinions, especially several more from him. Fortunately her
surgery was successful, and our discussion led to the poem of the same name.

As I write this I am starting to understand a few things. One, there are stories all around us. Two, you have to laugh a bit at life. And three write it down before you forget.

Stars to Chase has taken four years to produce after **Thinking Upside Down**. It will probably take at least as long to do **The Hidden Things** if I ever get it done. But it will be written and maybe someday someone will publish it if I don't. And if they do, I know someone will laugh or smile or think a kind thought because of it. And that's enough reason to take a quiet walk and let your thoughts roam a bit. Take a look around and let the ideas come to you. Keep a notebook by your bed so when you dream of something you can write it down right away before it retreats back to your subconscious. I did that myself the other day and wrote a poem called "To Look Afar" which may be the title for a book even after **The Hidden Things**.

That's also how I got to write about "Spot the Talking Bug." I had a dream that a bug was spinning around and hitting me with a chain. I hit back and Spot was born. Well, I guess he died, but you know what I mean, don't you? No? Well, remember, it was just a stupid dream.

School poems! How exciting! My daughter didn't think she was good at math, but she got some good teachers and ended up with A's . Funny how that works. They didn't get to her before her frustrations led me to write "The Pythagorean Poem" and "The Algebra Poem". I wrote "The First Day Back" some years ago in August just as school was starting. I like it because you don't get the "twist" until the very last word of the poem! Students just stare when I finish that poem, but teachers pick up on it right away. All a matter of perspective, I suppose.

That gets me going on a little pet peeve of mine. I once heard a man say, "I am not interested in the truth. I am only interested in my perspective and the truth is not important!" He seemed to be right for a very long time because he was one of those who destroyed that dream I talked about earlier. But I believe that the truth is all-important and even though we each view it through our own life experience, truth does not depend on how we view it. I enjoy poetry because I find truth through it and because it helps me to understand how someone else might see the same truth and come to a different conclusion. And that's the truth! Believing in the truth has led me here, writing for you, and living with an exciting dream that I did not ever imagine! And that's the truth, too. It could not have happened without the good AND the difficult experiences of life as the following poem illustrates. It's a very personal poem, too, which is why I felt it belonged here in the notes instead of in the text.

STONE PILLARS

Stone pillars on a vacant lot,
A house and home that time forgot,
Alone now on this empty space
I must now my failure face.
Expectations far too great!
A young man fallen from their weight.
An older man with weary eyes
Looks for help from distant skies.
The young man called. It never came.

The old man fears the very same.
With fading hope he draws each breath
And looks afar, beyond his death.
With words he travels quick through time.
To the stars he hopes to climb!
The old man feared the young man dead
But lived in long lost dreams instead.
The expectations are long past
But he fulfills them, now, at last.

I hope I've fulfilled your expectations when you bought this book.

I like horses. (How's that for an artful transition?) I don't like to ride them, but I like to look at them in fields and on hillsides. I really like to look at the Clydesdales in the Grant's Farm pastures as I drive by. So it's only natural that I'd write a few horse poems, like "Blinders on Horses" and "Seven Horses" which is really about eight horses if you think of it but since you didn't I got away with naming the poems the way I wanted to. Sharon told me about the seven, I mean eight, horses and I wrote a poem. She's always seeing the most interesting things! (I hope she still thinks I'm interesting!) Maybe she'll see something interesting on her trip!

Did you catch the title of the book "Alfred the Elf" is reading? How about the author? My dad wrote a very complex book about advanced mathematics. Numbers talked to him, I think. My mom wrote several books about German artists of early Texas, some of who were our ancestors. And I thought I was being an original by writing books of my own. I'm just a big copycat! I'm glad my parents were good examples and hope I am, too.

I'm not a very good example when it comes to housework. "As Is" and "Clutter" were both inspired by my messy house, as was "The Biggest Vine". We get a letter from the neighborhood association every once in a while about our lawn, too. Maybe that's why they didn't make me poet laureate of Byrnes Mill.

My daughter Erin inspired "Cookies by a Zombie" although she'll deny it to the last. She read the unusual name of a store while we were driving and I thought she said "Cookies by a Zombie" so I repeated that to her. She just looked away and said I was weird. I read her the poem later and proved it, I think.

The brownies play a big role in my Christmas poems because they were a part of my dad's holiday when he was growing up. His family tradition was that the brownies decorated the tree the night before Christmas and kept the naughty list. If you were bad, you got coal and switches on Christmas morning! I only heard this tale as an adult. (Okay, I heard about the coal and switches part but I never got those. I did not!) I've enjoyed writing the brownies into my poems except for the first one called "Secrets of the - Shhhh!" which is in my book, **Don't Feed the Seagulls**. I don't think the brownies liked being "exposed" at first, but I hope they have gotten used to it. Hey, maybe they're the ones who keep calling the shopping channels on TV with my credit card! It's not me!

I really like "One Doggone Christmas" and almost put it in **O Christmas Treed!** a few years ago but Sharon didn't like it so I didn't. I slipped it in here and added the pictures, and I think she's going to let me get away with it. Imagine what life would be like if I had a real editor who didn't like my poems and tried to get me to change them. Yuck! Maybe self-publishing isn't so bad, after all! I had a hard time drawing the dog at first but I've come up with a nifty way to draw an animal if nothing else works. The "two moons" part was added a couple of days after the rest of the poem was written. It just didn't seem to be as good as it could be without something more.

The cats and the dog did have a part in the poem called "My Magic Carpet" and that reminds me I have to finish up here pretty quickly and get home to take the dog out so I don't have to take the carpet out instead. I suppose that's my cue. It has been a real pleasure writing for you and I hope this little exercise has been useful or entertaining for you.

After all, this book is for you, for whom no star is too far to reach!

Your friend,

Byron von Rosenberg

ALPHABETICAL LIST OF POEMS

A CAT WITH YARN

Yarn seems to make cats happy
Although I've never been one.
It does the same for me
Every time I spin one.
There's a certain happiness
When my mind is busy whirring.
I think cats must feel that way
Whenever they are purring.
And so I sit and write
With a smile upon my face
Undeterred by circumstance
Of poverty and place.
For somehow I find courage
That heretofore I lost
Much like the playful kitty
For whom the yarn is tossed.
Nothing else does matter
As much as chasing yarn
And before I know it
I'm well outside the barn.
And on a new adventure
I scamper like a cat
For as a writer nothing
Excites me as does that!